Life Is What You Make It, Nothing More...Nothing Less

The Faith-Fueled Formula for Real Results

Ray Borell II

Published by Ray Borell Publishing
First Edition – May 2025

ISBN (Paperback): 979-8-218-71300-3
ISBN (eBook): Not applicable (Amazon Kindle ASIN assigned upon publication)

Cover design: Ray Borell II with design contributions by Joni Deutschman
Cover layout and production: Joni Deutschman
Cover illustration: *Winking Smiley Face with X Eye*, created by Ray Borell II
Interior layout and formatting: Ray Borell II
Typography: Garamond (headings and body)

Unless otherwise noted, Scripture quotations are from the **King James Version of the Holy Bible** (public domain). Some passages have been adapted by the author for inclusive language and clarity, in alignment with the themes and purpose of this book.

Select chapter-opening quotes are the intellectual property of their respective authors and are used here under the **fair use** principle, with full acknowledgment provided at the time of quotation.

This work is nonfiction and reflects the author's personal experience, faith, and perspective. Readers are encouraged to seek professional or spiritual counsel as needed. The content is intended for **inspirational and educational purposes only**.

For more information, visit:
www.RayBorell.com

Dedication

To my incredible wife, Amy —
Your love, strength, and belief in me have been the foundation of everything I've built.
You are my greatest blessing and my constant reminder of grace.

And to my amazing children, Erica and Ethan —
May you always know that you are powerful, capable, and created for greatness.
This book is for you — and the world you'll help shape.

Acknowledgments

To all of my mentors, colleagues, friends, and family who believed in me — thank you.

Jonathan — I am grateful to call you my friend. Your encouragement has meant more than you know.

Steve and Luke at Lodestar Guidance — thank you for your support over the years.

Paul Weaver — for your guidance, your friendship, and the hours spent in deep conversation. I will always and forever be grateful.

And to every person who reminded me who I was when I forgot — this book carries your fingerprints.

You are your #1 best investment.

And your most valuable resource is time.

Invest and spend wisely.

"As a man thinketh in his heart, so is he."

— Proverbs 23:7

"This book won't change your life — you will."

— Ray Borell II

Table of Contents

Part 4: The Keys (Ask, Seek, Knock)

Part 5: Real Talk — Supporting the Blueprint

Part 6: Activation & Alignment

Reflection and Journaling Section

Part 4: The Keys (Ask, Seek, Knock)

Part 5: Real Talk — Supporting the Blueprint

Part 6: Activation & Alignment

Reflection and Journaling Section

Author's Note

The smiley face on this cover isn't polished. It's a little rough, a little off-center—just like life.

I designed it that way on purpose. The open circle reminds me (and hopefully you) to stay open—open to learning, growth, change, and healing. The "X" eye is life's way of letting us know it doesn't always play fair. We all take hits. We all carry scars. But the smile—that's not an accident. That's a choice.

Every day, we decide how we respond to the pain, the pressure, and the process. That smile is a reflection of what I've learned: that resilience isn't about pretending everything's fine—it's about standing in the mess and choosing to keep going anyway.

This book is my story. My truth. My journey through the fire and what I found on the other side. I hope something in it speaks to yours.

—Ray Borell II

How to Use This Book

This book isn't meant to just inspire you — it's meant to activate you.

Each chapter is built to move you forward: from awareness to action, from belief to breakthrough. You'll find real stories, spiritual truth, and simple tools to help you build a life of purpose and power.

Here's how to get the most out of it:

◆ Reflect & Respond

At the end of most chapters, you'll find a *Reflection & Journaling Prompt*. Don't rush past it. This is where the real growth happens — when you slow down and get honest with yourself. Write your answers. Speak them out loud. Sit with the truth.

◆ Use the Space

In the back of the book, there's a dedicated section titled *Journaling & Reflection: Make It Yours*. These pages are here for you to engage with what you're learning. Use them freely — or grab a separate notebook if you prefer more space.

◆ Declare Truth

Chapter 12 walks you through the power of affirmations. These aren't just feel-good phrases — they're a way to rewire your thinking and speak life into your day. Read them. Write them. Repeat them daily.

◆ Apply the Blueprint

Parts 3 and 4 walk you through a clear model: Vision, Faith, Action — then Ask, Seek, Knock. These aren't just concepts. They're a pattern. A spiritual system. Use them as a framework anytime you feel stuck, uncertain, or ready for what's next.

◆ Revisit Often

Don't treat this like a one-time read. This is a resource. A playbook. A reminder of who you are and what's possible when you align with your Creator. Come back to it as often as you need.

The truth is already in you.

This book is here to help you remember — and respond.

.

Introduction

Let's be honest — most people don't change because they read a book. They change because they decide to act on what they know.

This book is about that decision. It's about building a life intentionally — not by accident, not by default, not someday. But now.

Because life isn't something that just happens to you. **Life is what you make it. Nothing more. Nothing less**.

You'll learn why most goals fail — and how yours don't have to. You'll discover how to rewire your beliefs, how to use vision and faith as tools, and how to move through resistance when it shows up (because it will). You'll get a blueprint you can apply immediately. Simple. Powerful. Proven.

The life you want isn't "out there" waiting to be found. It's already within your reach — if you're willing to do the work.

If you're ready to stop waiting and start building...
Turn the page.
Let's go!

CHAPTER 1

Life Is What You Make It

The best way to predict your future is to create it.

— Abraham Lincoln

I recently spoke at an all-men's retreat on the incredible power we have within us and the purpose of setting goals. I shared my viewpoint with this group on all the amazing opportunities we have living in these magnificent times. Midway through, a gentleman kindly interrupted me: "What makes it so great? There isn't anything special about this generation. My grandfather was part of the greatest generation."

I nodded. I respected where he was coming from. That generation had men of true grit, values, and hard-earned character. But I wasn't totally convinced they were the greatest. I asked the group, "If that's true, where did all the good men go?"

That stirred the room. Voices chimed in with answers: fatherless homes, drugs, alcohol, lack of accountability. Valid points, but I challenged them: "If those things have always existed, what does that say about you? Do you have character? Morals? Values?"

The energy shifted. One man shouted, "Hell yeah, I do!"

I smiled. "Damn straight you do. Or you wouldn't be here."

That moment helped me prove the point: **greatness exists in every generation**. It just depends on your perspective.

I continued. "What about biblical times? What about the warriors of Ancient Greece? Or the pioneers who crossed the Midwest in the 1800s? Were they any less great? Maybe, just maybe, we've been deceived. Maybe every generation is great in its own way, and progress is made because of that greatness."

Then I brought it home. "Living here in the U.S., we have so many opportunities. Wouldn't you agree? We can work hard, imagine, be creative, start businesses, and build whatever future we want. We have access to all the knowledge in the world at our fingertips. No generation before us had this kind of access."

Everyone was nodding now.

So I asked them one last question:

"If we live in amazing times, in an amazing country, with amazing opportunities... then why doesn't everyone grow up to live an amazing life?"

And then I told them what I'm about to tell you:

It's because of Limiting Beliefs.

Limiting beliefs are silent thieves. They rob people of their potential before they even get started. This is something that perplexed me for many years and I had to understand why. I spent over a decade studying success, mindset, and behavior, trying to answer this one simple question: Why do some people win at life while others stay stuck?

Henry Ford said it best: "Whether you think you can or think you can't, you're right."

Most people don't fail because they lack talent or opportunity. They fail because they don't believe it's possible for them.

Let me be real with you. I didn't grow up with a silver spoon. My mom abandoned me when I was five. My dad was an alcoholic. I had no direction. By middle school, I was already smoking and drinking. By high school, I was deep into drugs—and eventually, I dropped out.

But today? I've helped lead multi-million-dollar companies, own a real estate business, partnered in online ventures, and been married nearly 30 years—yes, that's an accomplishment. I live in the home I dreamed of, drive the truck I want, and live the life I once only imagined.

What changed?

I did.

I stopped being a victim. I stopped pointing fingers at my past and started owning my future. I went to work on myself.

Here's what I learned:

You may not control what happens to you, but you do control how you respond.

And if you want something different, you have to believe something different.

Because belief is the root of it all.

If you take nothing else from this book, I want you to take this:

You have the power to change your life, but you have to believe it first.

I have a short story I want to share with you about a gentleman named Roger Bannister.

Prior to 1952 the common belief on earth was that it was not humanly possible to run the mile in less than 4 minutes. It had never been done before, therefore the common belief on this planet was that man could not break the 4-minute mile barrier. Then a young man named Roger Bannister came along and broke the 4-minute mile barrier. Now what makes this story so interesting is that by the end of the week someone else broke it and by the end of that year 6 more people broke it. To this day more than 10,000 people have broken it. What changed? I'll tell you what changed.

Each one of those people stepped onto that track with a new belief planted inside them: that the barrier wasn't physical — it was mental. One person's breakthrough gave permission for others to rise. It wasn't magic, and it wasn't luck. It was proof. Proof that limits are often just stories we've accepted as fact. And once someone rewrites the story, it opens the door for others to do the same.

So let me ask you this: What have you been told is impossible? What story have you accepted as truth that's holding you back? Whatever your dream is — protect it. Feed it. Refuse to let it die. And above all, believe that it's within reach. Not just for someone else, but for you. Because if the limit was made up, you can break it too.

So right now, get up. Go find a mirror. Look yourself dead in the eyes and say:

"Life is what you make it. Nothing more... nothing less."

Now say it again. Louder. With conviction. Like your future self is watching. Because they are.

CHAPTER 2

What You Believe, You Become

Whether you think you can, or you think you can't — you're right.

— Henry Ford

We've all been shaped — by our families, our environments, and our experiences.

Somewhere along the way, whether we realized it or not, we started to form beliefs about who we are, what we're capable of, and what life is supposed to be.

Those beliefs?

They became the lens through which we see the world — and ourselves.

And most people never stop to question them.

We often assume what we believe is truth. But in reality, many of those beliefs were never ours to begin with.

The Power of Programming

The subconscious will accept whatever you give it. It doesn't filter.

It doesn't decide what's true or false — it simply accepts what's repeated.

That's why the Jesuits famously said,

"Give me a child until the age of seven, and I will show you the man."

From birth, we are being programmed.

Our primary caretakers — parents, grandparents, teachers — shape our earliest understanding of the world.

They plant the seeds that grow into beliefs.

But it doesn't stop with them.

We're influenced by:

- Friends and classmates

- Television and music

- Social media

- Culture

- And every authority figure we look up to

If we don't stand guard at the gates of our minds, our subconscious will accept all of it.

It has no choice.

As we grow, we *can* change — but here's the challenge: We're trying to change with the same mind that created the problem.

That's why real transformation is so hard.

Our beliefs become the lens through which we see life — and we can't fix what we can't see.
Most people never achieve what they truly want, not because they're lazy or incapable — but because they never stop to question the beliefs driving their behavior.

Worse, many people never even *hear* this truth.

Real Life: Chris's Story

Chris grew up hearing things like:
"That's not for people like us."
"We're not rich, and we never will be."
"Keep your expectations low and you won't be disappointed."

By the time he hit his thirties, Chris had dreams — but no confidence.
He'd talk himself out of every opportunity before it even started.

- "I'm not that type of person."

- "People like me don't make it."

- "What if I fail?"

But here's the shift: once Chris started questioning those thoughts — and realizing they weren't truth, just conditioning — things began to change.

He realized those beliefs were not facts. They were choices.

And choices can be rewritten.

Why This Matters

This chapter isn't just about psychology — it's about freedom.

Because once you realize that your beliefs are shaping your results, you can stop blaming outside circumstances and start doing something about it.

But it starts with getting honest.

We need to take inventory of where we are in life.

- How's your bank account?

- How's your health?

- How are your relationships?

- How do you feel when no one's around?

If your answer to any of those is "not where I want it to be," you don't need to beat yourself up.

You just need to be willing to admit: *maybe there's something I've been believing that isn't serving me.*

Your results are always an expression of your level of awareness.

Thought → Feeling → Action → Result

Let's break this down:

- A thought triggers an emotion.

- That emotion creates a feeling.

- That feeling drives an action.

- That action leads to a result.

- And that result reinforces the original thought.

    It's a loop — and it all starts with belief.

The same thought, repeated often enough, becomes a belief. Your beliefs shape your perception. And your perception becomes your reality.

Thoughts become things. What you focus on, you move toward. What you look for, you will find.

Common Limiting Beliefs

These don't always shout — sometimes they whisper quietly in the background:

In money:

- "I'm just not good with finances."
- "We'll always struggle."
- "Rich people are selfish."

In relationships:

- "People always leave."
- "I'm too damaged to be loved."
- "It's safer to be alone."

In health:

- "I'll always be like this."
- "I don't have the discipline."
- "It's too late to change."

In self-worth:

- "I'm not good enough."
- "I don't deserve success."
- "This is just who I am."

The Breakthrough

Here's the truth:

- You can change.

- You're not stuck.

- You are God's highest form of creation.

- You are not your programming — unless you choose to stay there.

Neville Goddard once said:

"You are only limited by weakness of attention and poverty of imagination."

That's why awareness is everything.

When you begin to question your beliefs — when you take inventory of your life and face what's really there — you open the door to something new.

Your results are not random — they are reflections of what you believe about yourself and what's possible.

Reflection and Journaling Prompt: What Have You Been Believing?

Take a moment to pause and reflect. No pressure — just truth.

Ask yourself:

- What do I believe about success, money, love, or health?

- Where did those beliefs come from?

- Are they helping me — or holding me back?

- What would I be capable of if I believed something better?

Take the time to sit with these questions.

Write your answers down. Don't rush this part.

This is where transformation begins.

You were not created to live limited.

The beliefs you've carried may have shaped your past, but they don't have to define your future.

You are capable of change — and it begins now.

Change your beliefs, and everything else follows.

CHAPTER 3

Rewiring Your Mind — The Science of Belief

Change your thoughts and you change your world.
— Norman Vincent Peale

Most of your beliefs were formed long before you knew you had a choice.

As children, we're in a **highly suggestible state** — soaking in everything like a sponge.

What you hear… what you're told… what you experience… it all gets stored.

And unless you intentionally rewrite the program, it runs quietly in the background — for the rest of your life.

That's not dramatic. That's just how the brain works.

Early Beliefs Become Your Operating System

If someone told you, "Money is hard to come by," "You're not good enough," or "That's not for people like us,"

Your subconscious didn't argue — it simply **accepted it as truth.**

This becomes your **internal narrative**. And once it's set, your mind starts working to reinforce it — without even realizing it.

Enter the **Reticular Activating System (RAS).**

Your Mind's Filter: The Reticular Activating System

The RAS is like a filter in your brain that decides what information gets through and what gets blocked out.
It lets in only what it believes is **important or relevant** — and how does it know what's relevant?

Whatever you **consistently think about, expect, and believe**.

So if your early beliefs were limiting, guess what your RAS does?

It starts looking for everything around you to **prove you right**.

You believe life is hard? Your brain will help you see struggle everywhere.
You believe people can't be trusted? Your RAS will highlight every betrayal.
You believe success is for "other people"? It'll make sure you feel like an outsider.

And that's the trap:

The same filter that could unlock growth... is **now reinforcing your limitations**.

Good News: Neuroplasticity is on Your Side

Here's the turning point: **your brain is not fixed.**

Through a process called **neuroplasticity**, your brain can create entirely new neural pathways — even in adulthood.

Every time you choose a new thought... speak a new truth... or take a different action...
You begin to **weaken the old pathways** and **build new ones**.

But to do this, you need to retrain both your thoughts and your RAS.

It's not just about changing your thinking — it's about creating **repetition strong enough** to rewire your brain's filter.

Real Life: Why You See What You Believe

Ever think about buying a certain kind of car — and then suddenly you see it everywhere?

That's not a sign from the universe. That's your **RAS** saying, "Oh, this matters now. Let me show you more of it."

Your brain is constantly scanning your environment for what's "important" — and if you keep thinking, *"I'm not enough,"* or *"Nothing ever works out for me,"*...

Your RAS will keep reinforcing that belief.

But if you begin thinking, *"God is for me,"* or *"I'm learning to succeed,"*
Then slowly, your filter starts to shift.

You're Not Stuck — You're Just Running an Old Program

This isn't about willpower.
This is about awareness.

You're not broken — you're just operating on beliefs that no longer serve you.

The truth is, you can change your life.
But you have to change your belief system first.

Because what you believe determines what you focus on.
What you focus on, your RAS amplifies.
And what gets amplified becomes your reality.

Repetition Is the Gateway

This is where transformation begins.

What you repeat, you reinforce.
And what you reinforce, you start to believe.

This is why affirmations, declarations, and visualizations aren't hype — they're tools.
You're not trying to lie to yourself — you're trying to retrain your brain.

And the brain learns through repetition.

So How Do You Rewire Your Mind?

Here's a simple, powerful process:

---

1. Identify the Limiting Belief

Get brutally honest:

- "I'm not smart enough."

- "I'll never get ahead."

- "I'm not worthy of love."

- "I can't change."

Write it down. Speak it out loud. Face it.
You can't fix what you refuse to name.

2. Challenge it With Truth

Where did it come from? Is it even true?

Find a scripture or empowering belief that contradicts it. Speak it. Own it.

Example:
Old belief: "I always mess things up."
New truth: "I am learning. God's grace is enough. I can grow and get better."

3. Repeat it Daily

Rewiring requires repetition.

- Say your new belief out loud, every morning.

- Write it down multiple times.

- Feel it emotionally when you speak it.

- Visualize yourself living it.

Every repetition weakens the old path and strengthens the new one.

And as you do this, your RAS will begin to shift — showing you new evidence to support your new identity.

4. Take Aligned Action

Don't just speak it — walk it.

Your actions reinforce your identity.
Even a small step builds momentum.

- Start the workout.

- Apply for the opportunity.

- Speak the truth over yourself when no one else does.

That's how change becomes permanent.
Action turns belief into experience — and experience becomes
evidence.

This Is Not About Hype

This is about reprogramming the system that's been shaping
your life without your permission.

It's about replacing broken programming with the truth of
who you really are:

A child of God.
A creator.
A conqueror.

You have power.

You have purpose.

And you have the ability to create a life that reflects both.

The secret isn't out there — it's already inside you.
Now let's bring it to life.

Thoughts become patterns.

Patterns become beliefs.

Beliefs shape your life.

So start where all change begins — with your mind.

You have power. You have purpose. And you have the ability to create a life that reflects both.

The secret isn't out there. It's already inside you.

Now let's bring it to life.

Reflection & Journaling Prompt

Take a moment to reflect — not just with your mind, but with your heart.

Ask yourself:

• What belief has been holding me back the most?

• Where did that belief come from — and is it even true?

- What truth do I want to begin reinforcing starting today?

- What small, aligned action can I take to support this new belief?

Remember — repetition builds the pathway.

Speak it. Write it. Live it.

CHAPTER 4

The Power of Interpretation — And the Risk of Misunderstanding

We don't see things as they are, we see them as we are.

— Anaïs Nin

Every day, in relationships and conversations, we see how easily meaning can get lost. A wife says one thing, her husband hears another. Neither is wrong, but both walk away with two different versions of the truth.

Or have you ever played that game where a message is whispered from one person to the next — and by the end of the line, it barely resembles the original?

That's how meaning can shift over time.
Not because someone intended to distort it…
but because language, tone, and context change the moment a message leaves its original form.

Communication isn't just about what's said. It's about what's understood.

And this isn't just a relationship problem. It's a human problem.

We've seen how thoughts shape beliefs, and beliefs shape reality.

But where do those original thoughts come from?

Many are passed to us through teachings, traditions, and even sacred texts.

And while the Word of God is unchanging, human interpretation can sometimes cloud what was always meant to be clear.

Now imagine that happening with the most influential text in history — the Bible.

The Bible was originally written in Hebrew and Aramaic, then later translated into Greek, and finally into English — most famously by William Tyndale in the 1500s. Every stage of translation introduced new interpretations, new word choices, and even cultural biases.

Think about how stories change when they're retold. Maybe a key word gets left out. Maybe the tone shifts. Maybe someone emphasizes a different part of the message. Eventually, you've got a completely different takeaway — all from the same original story.

So we have to ask:

Is it possible some original meanings of the Bible were lost in translation?

Could centuries of interpretation by men — often with political or religious agendas — have shifted the message?

The truth is, **perspective shapes everything**.
And when we read Scripture, we bring our own biases, filters, and personal experiences into the mix.

That doesn't mean the Bible isn't true. In fact, it further supports the idea that **within its passages are hidden keys** — keys that may have been mistranslated, misunderstood, or simply left out of modern teaching.

It means we need to be **humble and open** in how we read it. We need to seek understanding — not just recite tradition.

Real Life: Misinterpretation Can Shape a Life

Marcus grew up hearing sermons about humility — but what he internalized was, *"Don't stand out. Don't dream too big. Don't outshine others."*

So he dimmed his light. For years.

But something felt off. And when he finally started digging into Scripture himself, he saw that humility wasn't about shrinking — it was about surrendering *ego*, not *potential*.

That shift didn't just change how Marcus thought.

It changed how he lived.

The Hidden Message That Never Changed

The deeper message of the Bible — the one that transcends language and culture — is this:

You are more powerful than you think.

You are made in the image of the Creator.

You are not here to live small.

You're here to **create**, to **grow**, and to **become**.

Jesus himself said in Luke 17:21,

"The kingdom of God is within you."

That means heaven isn't just some far-off place.

It's a **state of awareness**.

A **mindset**.

A life aligned with truth.

Because the real secret might not be buried in mystery — it might just be buried under **years of misinterpretation**.

And now?

Now you're uncovering it.

What if We've Been Given the Power to Create?

This is not new age fluff.
This is ancient truth — buried under centuries of fear, guilt, and religious confusion.

When Jesus said *"The kingdom of God is within you,"* He wasn't being poetic.
He was giving you a blueprint.

He was saying:
Heaven isn't just a destination — it's a dimension. A mindset. A spiritual reality you carry with you.

And it's within your reach.
Right now. Not someday. Not if you're good enough. Now.

Interpretation Isn't Just About Words — It Shapes Identity

Here's the real danger:
If we misunderstand the message, we misunderstand **who we are**.

- Instead of creators, we see ourselves as victims.

- Instead of partners with God, we live like powerless spectators.

- Instead of living from divine design, we hide in religious guilt.

But here's the truth:

You don't need to abandon your faith to claim your power.

You don't need to leave God behind to believe you were born to build something great.

You are powerful **because** of God.

You were made in the Creator's image — **to create.**

Real Life: Reclaiming the Message

Janelle ran a business but kept hitting a wall. She believed success might make her "worldly" or less spiritual. She was afraid of crossing some invisible line.

But as she studied Scripture more closely, she saw stories of stewardship, multiplication, and kingdom expansion. She realized God wasn't opposed to growth — God was the source of it.

Now her business isn't just profitable — it's purpose-filled. Because she stopped separating faith from action and started interpreting Scripture through the lens of partnership, not passivity.

Here's the Invitation

The real secret might not be buried in mystery — it might just be buried under years of misinterpretation.

And now?

Now you're uncovering it.

So give yourself permission to read it again.

Ask the deeper questions:

• What does this verse really mean?

• Who was it written to?

• What truth might I have missed?

Because truth holds up under pressure.

And when you find it — the real truth — it won't shrink you.

It will set you free.

Reflection & Journaling Prompt

Let's bring it home. Your interpretation shapes your identity.

Ask yourself:

• Where have I misinterpreted something in a way that shrank my confidence or calling?

• What religious or cultural message did I receive that I now see differently?

• Where have I felt torn between faith and personal growth?

You weren't created to shrink. You were created to partner with your Creator — and build.

CHAPTER 5

Identity, Purpose, and the Power Within

At the center of your being you have the answer; you know
who you are and you know what you want.

— Lao Tzu

Before we talk strategy, we have to talk identity.
Because without knowing **who you are**, you'll never fully walk into
what you're meant to do.

So many people are searching for purpose, chasing titles or
achievements just to feel like they matter. But your identity doesn't
come from the world. It doesn't come from your past, your
paycheck, or your popularity.

It comes from your Creator.

You Were Made in the Creator's Image

Genesis 1:27 says:

"So God created mankind in God's own image, in the image
of God the Creator made them; male and female God created them."

That verse isn't just theology — it's identity.

You were made in the image of a Creator.

That means creativity, boldness, wisdom, and purpose are woven into your design.

You weren't created to play small, conform, or just survive.
You were created to build. To express. To contribute.
You carry the DNA of divine power — the ability to think, imagine, choose, and create.

Real Life: From Lost to Leading

Eric spent years drifting from job to job, never really settling. He didn't feel fulfilled, but he also didn't think he had any specific calling. One night, in frustration, he asked God, *"Why am I even here?"*

It wasn't a sermon or a lightning bolt that gave him clarity. It was a moment of silence — followed by a thought: *"You've been helping people your whole life. You just didn't see it as purpose."*

He looked back and saw that even in jobs he didn't love, he was always mentoring someone, solving problems, encouraging others.

That was the thread.
Once he saw it, things changed.
He leaned into coaching. He started building a business helping others discover their own purpose. And in doing so, he found his own.

Your Purpose Isn't "Out There" — It's Within

Romans 8:28 reminds us:

"And we know that in all things God works for the good of those who love the Creator, who have been called according to God's purpose."

Your purpose isn't something you stumble into by accident. It's something that's been **woven into your wiring from the beginning**.

It's not always about a big career move or a dramatic calling. Sometimes, it's in how you listen.
How you love.
How you lead in the small things — and grow into the big ones.

Real Life: When the Role Doesn't Define the Calling

Denise spent years as a stay-at-home mom. She believed in raising her kids well, but deep down, she sometimes felt "less than" the women around her who had jobs, platforms, or influence.

Then one day, one of her adult children told her, "You're the reason I know who I am. You gave me identity."

That hit her hard — because it reminded her that **purpose isn't always loud or visible**.

She wasn't just "a mom."

She was a mirror. A builder of belief. A life-shaper.

Sometimes, the most powerful purpose looks ordinary to the world — but heaven calls it priceless.

The World Says, "Find Yourself."

God Says, "You Were Already Chosen."

You don't have to earn your value.
You don't have to prove your worth.
You don't have to become someone else to be powerful.

You were **already chosen**.
You were **already equipped**.
And nothing about you is accidental — you carry something the world needs.

So ask yourself:

- Who does God say I am?

- What fires me up — not just emotionally, but spiritually?

- Where do I feel pulled to make an impact?

- What pain have I lived through that I could now help others navigate?

Because your purpose is often hiding in plain sight.

In your passions.

In your past.

In the places where your joy and your scars intersect.

You don't need to chase significance.
You just need to **recognize who you already are** — and begin living from that truth.

That's the foundation.

That's the key.

And that's where the Blueprint begins to unlock everything else.

Reflection & Journaling Prompt

Take a moment to get quiet. No pressure. Just you and the truth.

Ask yourself:

- What labels have I accepted that don't align with who God says I am?

- Have I been defining my worth by what I do — or by who I am?

- Where in my life do I feel the most alive, the most useful, or the most at peace?

- What do others often come to me for? (That's often a clue.)

- Is there something I've been disqualifying myself from — that I actually feel called to?

  And now ask God:

- "Show me who I really am."

- "Reveal what You've placed in me that I've ignored or underestimated."

- "Help me see my past through the lens of purpose."

You don't need to figure it all out right now.
But you do need to begin seeing yourself clearly.

You are not random.
You are not broken.
You are not late.

You were created on purpose — for a purpose.

CHAPTER 6

Vision. Faith. Action. The Biblical Blueprint for Change

Vision without action is merely a dream. Action without vision just passes the time. Vision with action can change the world.
—Joel A. Barker

If life is truly what you make it — nothing more and nothing less — then we need a reliable way to make it. A roadmap. A set of principles to build from. And that blueprint? It's found in the Bible.

Now, I'm not a theologian, and I don't pretend to be. But I do believe scripture is far more practical than we give it credit for. Beyond its spiritual depth, it offers a clear process — a divine system for creating the life we desire. And it begins with this foundational trio:

Vision. Faith. Action.

Let's break it down.

Vision — See It Before You Can Build It

Proverbs 29:18 says, *"Where there is no vision, the people perish."* Without a plan, without direction, without goals — people drift. They settle into routines, not purpose.

Think about it: if we have no goals, we're likely going nowhere. We wake up, go to work, come home, eat dinner, scroll our phone, fall asleep... and then do it all over again tomorrow. Days turn into months, months into years — and suddenly three years have gone by with no real progress. In fact, maybe we've slipped backward. Maybe we've gained weight, lost money, or seen our relationships suffer — and we can't even explain why.

This is what life looks like without vision.

If we want a better life (and we all do), we must have goals — and we must be actively working on them. One quote says: *"If you're not growing, you're dying."* That's what goals do: they force us to grow. To move. To improve.

Some say it's too much work. But let's be honest — that's an excuse. And excuses leave people stuck: fat, broke, lonely, and unhappy.

How do I know? Because that was me.

Life is hard. I get that. But not working on yourself is even harder. We get fooled into believing we can put things off, that someday we'll "get to it." But every day that passes is a missed opportunity to move closer to the life we were meant to live.

Procrastination is a killer of dreams.

And deep down, nobody wants to reach the end of their life knowing they could have done better.

Most of us do have a vision, somewhere deep down: the kind of house we want, the car we want to drive, the relationship we dream of, the career we hope for. But what we need is a shift in perspective — to realize that goals are just vision in motion. Short-term goals, stacked and repeated, will lead us to the long-term vision we carry in our heart.

As Jim Rohn once said, *"There are two ways to look at the future: one with apprehension, the other with anticipation."*

So ask yourself: How do most people you know look at their future?

Most look with fear, stress, or doubt. Why? Because they haven't designed it.

They're walking through life with fingers crossed, hoping things will just "work out." And I'll be honest — even the most sincere, faith-filled saint with their fingers crossed won't get far without vision and aligned action.

I've tried. It doesn't work.

Having a vision is not just about seeing with your eyes. It's about seeing with your mind. It's engaging your imagination — that divine spark within us that allows us to dream and design our future. Vincent van Gogh said, *"I dream my painting, and then I paint my dream."* That's the essence of vision.

Faith — Believe It Before You See It

Hebrews 11:1 says, *"Now faith is the substance of things hoped for, the evidence of things not seen."* Faith is the bridge between your vision and your reality. It's what allows you to act, even when there's no physical evidence — yet.

Faith isn't blind hope. It's conviction. It's saying, *"Even though I don't see it right now, I believe it's already mine."* Faith fuels persistence. It keeps you moving when things get hard. And they will get hard.

Faith is more than just believing — it's trusting. Trusting God's timing. Trusting the unseen process. Trusting that what the Creator placed in your heart wasn't random, but divine.

And here's the truth: if the vision really came from God, it will require faith. You won't have all the answers. You won't have full control. That's on purpose. Because faith is what grows us. It keeps us dependent on the Creator — not just on our plans.

Hebrews 11, often called the Faith Hall of Fame, lists heroes who changed the world — not because they had guarantees, but because they acted on a word from God. Noah built the ark before it ever rained. Abraham left his home not knowing where he was going. Moses stepped into the Red Sea while the water was still there.

Faith is uncomfortable. It requires movement before evidence. But that's the point.

Real faith says: *"Even if I don't see it yet, I'll walk like it's already mine."*

That kind of faith unlocks doors. It changes atmospheres. It pulls the spiritual into the physical.

And here's what I've learned:

If your vision doesn't require faith, it's probably too small.

Faith makes you bold. Not reckless — but obedient. It helps you take steps when fear says "wait." And it reminds you that even in the silence, God is working.

But I also understand this: faith can be shaken. Especially in the middle of a storm — when it feels like everything is falling apart, when it looks like things won't work out, and when you're tempted to give up.

I've been there. We all have.

But remember this truth: just like the seasons, this too shall pass. Even after winter comes the spring. And no matter how dark the sky gets, every storm eventually breaks.

The key is to remain faithful during those times. To hold the line. To trust the process. Because that's when your faith is being refined. And that's when your breakthrough is often closer than you think.

Action — Do the Work

James 2:17 puts it plainly: *"Faith without works is dead."*

You can have the clearest vision and the strongest belief, but if you don't act — nothing changes.

Action is what gives life to your vision and fuel to your faith.

This is where a lot of people get stuck. They dream, they pray, they believe... but they don't move.

They wait for the perfect moment, the perfect plan, or the perfect feeling.

We can't just sit around hoping, praying, and thinking positive thoughts. Faith isn't passive. It moves. It builds. It pursues.

The Bible also teaches us in Galatians 6:7, *"Be not deceived; God is not mocked: for whatsoever a man soweth, that shall he also reap."*

This is what I call God's Universal Law of Compensation — the spiritual version of what science calls the Law of Cause and Effect.

For every effect, there is a cause. Nothing happens by accident. Whether we understand the reason or not, there is always one.

And here's the thing — you don't have to believe in a law for it to work.

You don't have to believe in gravity. But if you walk off a tenth-story balcony, you're going to hit the ground — and that'll be all she wrote. Gravity doesn't care if you believe in it or not. It just works.

The same is true with sowing and reaping. With cause and effect. With action and result.

Your vision is the cause — the seed — planted through the use of your imagination.
Your action, fueled by faith, is the labor — the work — that produces the harvest.

The Farmer's Principle

Think of your goals like a farmer thinks about a harvest. He doesn't just pray over the field and hope something grows. He gets to work. He tills the soil, plants the seeds, waters them, protects them, and waits.

He knows the harvest is coming — but only if he does his part.

The farmer doesn't plant corn on Monday and go looking for a full crop on Tuesday. He understands the law of process. That growth takes time. That seeds grow beneath the surface before they ever break through the topsoil.

But the harvest always responds to the seed — and to the faithfulness of the farmer.

Your life works the same way.

Your vision is the seed.
Your faith is the belief that it will grow.
And your action is the watering, the tending, the cultivating — even when you don't see anything yet.

Just as action must be taken in the Farmer's principle, the same applies to any goal. Any dream. **Action must be taken.**

Real Life: Small Moves, Big Momentum

Tina had been dreaming about writing a book for five years. She had notes in her phone, scraps of ideas in journals, and half-written pages on her laptop. But she always felt stuck — waiting for the "perfect time" to start.

One day, she decided to do something different. She wrote one sentence.

That sentence led to a paragraph. That paragraph turned into a page. And over the next 90 days, those small daily actions turned into her finished manuscript.

It didn't take a giant leap. It took consistent movement.

Action is the thread that pulls it all together — it's what makes the invisible visible, and the future possible. But not just any action will do.

There must be specific action. Purposeful action. And this is where we return to the foundation of truth — the Word of God.

The Keys are in Matthew 7:7

In Matthew 7:7, Jesus gives us the formula:

"Ask, and it will be given to you; seek, and you will find; knock, and it will be opened to you."

It's not just a spiritual idea — it's a practical formula and the hidden keys to achieving your dreams.

Reflection & Journal Prompt: Aligning with the Blueprint

- Where am I lacking vision right now?

- What have I been asking or praying for — but not truly believing?

- What's one small action I can take this week toward my vision?

- Am I waiting for conditions to be perfect — or am I willing to start now?

Your vision is the seed.

Your faith is the fuel.

Your action is the water.

Plant it. Believe it. Move on it.

The harvest is coming.

CHAPTER 7

Ask — Clarity and Courage

You get in life what you have the courage to ask for.

— Oprah Winfrey

In Matthew 7:7, Jesus says: **"Ask, and it will be given to you; seek, and you will find; knock, and it will be opened to you."**

This is more than just a nice spiritual saying.
It's a **principle. A pattern. A promise.**

But here's the catch: most people don't ask.
Or they ask passively. Vaguely. Without clarity. Without courage.
And then they wonder why nothing changes.

Let's be honest — asking can feel uncomfortable.
It takes vulnerability. It requires ownership.
It means admitting, *"There's something more I want, and I haven't seen it yet."*

But asking is the first step toward transformation.
You can't receive what you're unwilling to request.
And here's the kicker: of all the people you will encounter in life, the

most important person you must be asking questions to — is yourself.

Because the quality of your life is directly tied to the quality of questions you ask yourself.

When you ask better questions, you get better answers.

When you get better answers, you make better decisions.

And better decisions create a better life.

Ask Like You Mean It

One of the biggest mistakes people make is asking too generally:

- "God, bless me."

- "Help me be successful."

- "I want a better life."

But what does that actually mean?

Vague goals get vague results.
Specific goals open specific doors.

You've got to ask **intelligently. Intentionally.**
Ask with clarity and detail.

Don't just say, *"I want a better relationship."*
Say: *"I want to build a marriage where we talk openly, pray together, and show up for each other daily."*

Don't just say, *"I want to be healthy."*

Say: *"I want to lose 25 pounds, feel energized every morning, and run a 5K in the next six months."*

Don't just say, *"I want to make more money."*

Say: *"I want to earn an extra $1,000 a month doing work that aligns with my values and strengths."*

That's how you activate the power of asking.

You give your intention something real to grab onto — and your brain something real to pursue.

The Mind Loves a Question

The human mind is built to answer questions.

The questions you ask yourself become the focus of your life.

Ask better questions.

You'll get better answers.

Don't be afraid to ask God for what you need, what you desire, or what's on your heart.

He's not offended by big dreams.

He's not intimidated by your requests.

In fact, **He invites them.**

James 4:2 says,

"You do not have because you do not ask."

Asking boldly shows you're aware of your value.

It's not arrogance — it's alignment with your potential.

It shows you trust the process. That you're ready to step up and participate in what's possible.

Real Life: What If the Answer Isn't No?

Brian had worked at the same job for ten years. He had a steady paycheck, benefits, and zero passion. Deep down, he wanted more — but he never really asked. He assumed the answer would be no. No opportunity. No time. No way it would work.

But one day, he sat down and got honest with himself. He wrote out exactly what he wanted — down to the hours, the income, the kind of work, and the impact it would have.

Then he prayed about it. Then he asked.

He asked his boss about new opportunities.

He asked a mentor for guidance.

He asked God for clarity — and doors started opening.

The answer wasn't no.

The answer was **waiting on him to ask**.

Ask with Boldness

To ask is to get clear.

To articulate what you really want.

To stop shrinking your desires and start speaking them aloud.

God honors bold requests — not arrogance, but confidence grounded in trust.

Asking opens the door to alignment.

It's where the vision starts taking shape in your life.

"You do not have because you do not ask God." — James 4:2

So let me ask you this:

What are you not asking for, simply because you've assumed the answer would be no?

Reflection & Journaling Prompt: Ask with Intention

- What specific area of your life have you been too vague about?

- What do you *really* want to ask for — in your health, relationships, finances, or calling?

- Are you playing small because you're afraid of disappointment?

Get specific.

Get honest.

Write it out.

Speak it aloud.

Ask like someone who knows they were made for more.

CHAPTER 8

Seek — Discover, Learn, Pursue

What you seek is seeking you.

— Rumi

"Seek, and you will find..." — Matthew 7:7 Asking is where it starts.

But seeking is where things begin to shift.

This is the stage where many people fall off. They pray, they ask, they journal — but they don't pursue. They expect answers to fall out of the sky, forgetting this truth:

What you're looking for is already out there.

But you have to go find it.

Everything you need already exists — the knowledge, the people, the opportunities, the tools. They're not waiting to be created. They're waiting to be discovered.

But discovery requires movement.

It requires seeking.

We live in the most resource-rich time in history. Never before has knowledge been this accessible:

- Books

- Podcasts

- YouTube

- Mentorship

- Masterclasses

- Online communities

- Faith-based teachers and personal development experts

You can literally learn anything.

Want to improve your finances, build a better marriage, grow spiritually, get healthy, or start a business?

It's out there.

But it won't come find you.

Seek with Intention

Proverbs 4:7 says:

"Wisdom is the principal thing; therefore get wisdom: and with all thy getting get understanding."

Not just more information.

But the *right* information.

The kind that equips you to take action in faith and walk with clarity.

Seeking is about becoming a student again.

It means reading the book. Watching the class. Showing up. Asking

questions. Being humble enough to admit you don't know it all —
and hungry enough to find out what you don't know yet.

Real Life: From Confusion to Calling

After years of feeling stuck in his 9-to-5, David realized he
was deeply unfulfilled. He had asked God for guidance countless
times, but nothing seemed to shift.

Until one day, his pastor said something that hit him:

"Sometimes God doesn't give you the answer — He gives
you the search."

So David got curious. He started listening to podcasts during
his commute. He read books on calling and purpose. He reached out
to people doing work that inspired him.

One conversation led to another, and eventually, he met a
mentor who challenged him to pursue coaching — something David
had never considered but had a natural gift for.

Today, he's a certified coach, leading others through the same
journey that once left him feeling lost.

What changed?

He started seeking.
He didn't have it all figured out. But he moved anyway.
He searched. He showed up. He stayed curious and open to
possibilities.

And step by step, answers began to appear. Resources surfaced. New opportunities came into view.

That's what seekers do.

They move forward even when the path isn't fully clear — trusting that clarity comes through action, not before it.

Your Life Will Rise to the Level of Your Seeking

You can say you want change.

But if your time and attention say otherwise — it doesn't matter.

You will always move in the direction of what you seek.

If you seek entertainment, you'll find distraction.

If you seek comfort, you'll stay stuck.

But if you seek growth, wisdom, and alignment with your God-given vision?

You'll find a way forward — every time.

"Those who seek me diligently will find me." — Proverbs 8:17

Seeking is spiritual. It's mental. It's practical. It's the daily discipline of showing up for your growth — with purpose and pursuit.

It's not passive. It's active.

So seek knowledge.

Seek wisdom.

Seek mentors.

Seek feedback.

Seek your next step.

Seek God.

Seeking shows God — and yourself — that you're serious about the vision.

Because the promise is clear:

Seek — and you will find.

Reflection & Journaling Prompt

Pause and reflect. This is where the clarity you're seeking often starts to surface.

Ask yourself:

- What am I currently seeking with the most focus?

- Am I spending my time in alignment with what I say I want?

- What's one area I've been waiting for clarity — but haven't been actively pursuing it?

CHAPTER 9

Knock — Take Bold, Consistent Action

Opportunities don't happen. You create them.

— Chris Grosser

"Knock, and it will be opened to you." — Matthew 7:7
"To the one who knocks, the door will be opened." — Matthew
7:8

Knocking is where faith becomes movement.
You've asked. You've sought. Now you knock.

You knock on the door of opportunity.
On the hearts of others.
On your own resistance.
On the habits you need to build and the fears you need to break.

And you knock again and again — trusting that what you seek is already in motion.

Knocking Requires Persistence

This is where many people stop.

They ask once.

They try for a little while.

But when the first door doesn't open, they quit.

Take John, for example.

He's finally gotten clear on what he wants — to start his own business so he can spend more time with his family and build something he believes in.

He asks God for direction. He writes out his vision. He starts seeking advice, watching videos, learning everything he can. He even launches a website and offers his first product.

But after a couple of months... crickets.

Hardly anyone is buying. He's losing money. His friends don't seem to support him like he thought they would. And self-doubt starts creeping in.

He starts thinking:

"Maybe this isn't meant to be."

"Maybe I heard God wrong."

"Maybe I'm just not cut out for this."

And so he stops. He doesn't knock again. He lets the unopened door define him — instead of walking to the next one.

But here's the truth: it's not that the door was wrong — it's that he stopped knocking.

Knocking doesn't mean instant results.
It means showing up again and again, even when the door doesn't swing open on the first try.

But that's not knocking. That's tapping.

Persistence is the real secret.
This is where your belief gets tested.
Not in the asking. Not in the seeking.
But in the waiting — and the repeating.

You knock with your energy. Your effort. Your attitude.
Your habits.
You knock by showing up daily. With consistency. With resolve.

One Closed Door Doesn't Mean Stop

Listen — one closed door doesn't mean it's over.

Too many people take a "no" as a final answer.

But sometimes the door doesn't open because it's not your door.
Or it's not your time.
Or you're meant to grow stronger through the process.

One closed door is not the end of the story.

Take Barbara.

She's been working hard in her job for years — showing up early, staying late, going above and beyond.

She finally applies for a big promotion she's been eyeing, believing this is her moment.

She prays, prepares, interviews… and then she gets passed over.

Crushed, she starts to wonder:
"What was all this for?"
"Why did I even try?"
"Is this all there is?"

But what she doesn't know is that the rejection was actually redirection.

The skills she sharpened, the leadership she developed, the persistence she built — those things weren't wasted. They were seeds.

And a few months later, a new opportunity opens — one she never would've seen if she hadn't grown through the last one.

You just go to the next door.

And the next.

And the next.

And eventually — the right one opens.

You don't stop knocking because you got turned down.

You keep on keepin' on.

That's where the breakthrough lives.

Knock With Action and Intention

Knocking is more than just hoping. It's doing.

You apply. You reach out. You build. You improve. You pitch. You create.

You put yourself in position to receive what you've asked for and sought after.

Even when it feels repetitive. Even when it's slow.
You stay in the rhythm: **Ask. Seek. Knock.**

Knocking is action with expectation.
It's saying, "I'm not leaving until something happens."
It's belief that refuses to fold.

The Rhythm of the Blueprint

Ask. Seek. Knock.

It's not random.
It's a **pattern**.
A **holy rhythm** of vision, belief, and movement.

When you commit to this rhythm, your life starts to shift. Not always instantly — but always intentionally.

Reflection & Journaling Prompt

Take a moment to reflect and write:

- Where have I been "tapping" instead of truly knocking?

- What area of my life needs more consistent, intentional action?

- Am I interpreting closed doors as signs to quit — or opportunities to grow?

- What's one specific "door" I will knock on this week?

Most People Don't Finish the Cycle

Most people don't finish the cycle.

But **you're not most people.**

You keep going. You keep asking. You keep seeking.

And most of all — you keep knocking.

Because you know the promise:

"To the one who knocks, the door will be opened."

Together, **Ask, Seek, and Knock** create a rhythm of intentional living.

A spiritual pattern for real-world results — and the keys to unlocking your dreams.

CHAPTER 10

Discipline, Focused Attention, and Persistence

Success is the sum of small efforts repeated day in and day out.
— Robert Collier

We've talked about belief, identity, purpose, and strategy. We've explored the Biblical Blueprint of Vision, Faith, and Action — along with the 3 keys: Ask, Seek, and Knock.

But here's the truth:

None of it matters without discipline.

Discipline is what turns desire into reality.
It's doing what needs to be done even when you don't feel like it.
It's making choices today that your future self will thank you for.

And it's not about perfection — it's about **consistency**.

Anyone can be motivated for a day.
But the people who win — who actually create lives of freedom and impact — are the ones who show up again and again, even when it's boring, uncomfortable, or inconvenient.

Why Small Wins Matter

That's where small wins come in.

When you set small, manageable goals and consistently achieve them, you build momentum.
You build **trust with yourself**. And that's where confidence is born — not from hype, but from **follow-through**.

Galatians 6:9 reminds us:

"Let us not grow weary in doing good, for at the proper time we will reap a harvest if we do not give up."

You may not see results right away.
That's okay. Stay planted. Keep watering.
Your harvest is coming.

A Powerful Shift in Mindset

- Don't chase motivation. Chase **momentum**.

- Don't wait for inspiration. Build a **routine**.

- Don't let your feelings dictate your discipline.
  Let your **vision** lead your action.

Discipline doesn't always feel good. It's not glamorous. It's rarely fun in the moment.

But it's the **bridge between where you are and where you're going**.

Nick Saban, the former University of Alabama football coach — arguably the greatest college football coach of all time — once said:

"There are two pains in life. The pain of discipline and the pain of disappointment.
If you can handle the pain of discipline, then you'll never have to deal with the pain of disappointment."

Let that sink in.

Living with the weight of what could've been?
That might just be the most painful experience on this earth.

And I'm not willing to accept that for my life.
I don't think you want that for yours either.
Not for you — and not for the people you love.

Discipline isn't punishment — it's protection.
It protects your potential.
It builds momentum.
It builds character.
It's how you become the person your vision requires you to be.

Focused Attention: The Steering Wheel of Discipline

Next comes **focused attention** — the steering wheel of discipline.

Where you place your attention determines where your life goes.

James Allen, the father of modern self-development, wrote in *As a Man Thinketh*:

"A man's mind may be likened to a garden, which may be intelligently cultivated or allowed to run wild...

If no useful seeds are put into it, then an abundance of useless weed-seeds will fall therein."

What we focus on grows.

Earl Nightingale said it best:

"We become what we think about."

Your attention is like sunlight.

Whatever you shine it on... grows.

In today's world, attention is under constant attack — notifications, distractions, endless scrolling.

But the most successful, fulfilled people all share one trait: **they know how to focus.**

They give their time, energy, and thoughts to what truly matters.

Colossians 3:2 reminds us:

"Set your minds on things above, not on earthly things."

You can't control everything around you.

But you can control what you **choose to focus on**.

Ask yourself:

- What am I giving my energy to?

- Are my habits and routines aligned with my vision?

- Is my attention building my future — or draining it?

Because where your focus goes, your energy flows.

Real Life: The Power of Focus — Meet Eric

Eric had a vision to start his own fitness coaching business — not just for income, but to help people heal. But between his 9-to-5 job, family responsibilities, and a flood of social media distractions, he could never seem to "find the time."

Everything changed when he got intentional.

He started waking up 30 minutes earlier. Turned off his notifications. Created a "focus zone" during his evenings to build his side hustle.

Six months later? His coaching program was live.

A year later? He left his day job.

What changed? Not his talent. Not his passion.

His focus.

Persistence: Self-Discipline in Motion

And finally — **persistence**.

Persistence is the result of discipline.

It's **self-discipline in motion** — the ability to keep going in the midst of failure and setbacks.

And it's a vital characteristic for anyone chasing a meaningful goal.

Persistence isn't loud.

It's not flashy.

It's quiet, daily decisions.

It's praying when you feel dry. Showing up when you feel unseen. Working when no one is watching.

It's continuing **even when the results haven't shown up yet**.

It's trusting the process.

It's knowing the seed is still growing underground, even if you can't see it yet.

You must have a willingness to overcome in the face of adversity.

To keep on keepin' on.

Failure is not the end — it's part of the path.

Growth doesn't come in the comfort zone. It comes in the stretch zone. The faith zone. The persistence zone.

Here are a few of my favorite quotes that keep me going:

- "Energy and persistence conquer all things." — Benjamin Franklin

- "Paralyze resistance with persistence." — Woody Hayes

- "Persistence and determination alone are omnipotent." — Calvin Coolidge

Success doesn't always come to the smartest or most talented. But it will come to those who refuse to quit.

Persistence isn't just about grit.
It's also about **faith**.

Hebrews 10:36 reminds us:

"You need to persevere so that when you have done the will of God, you will receive what God has promised."

And Romans 5:3–4 says:

"We also glory in our sufferings, because we know that suffering produces perseverance; perseverance, character; and character, hope."

That's it.

This is the **real growth zone**.
Not the easy stuff. Not the highlight reel.
But the trenches.

That's where the Creator shapes you — and where your character becomes unshakable.

Reflection & Journaling Prompt

- Where in my life have I lacked discipline — and how has it cost me?

- What distractions are stealing my focus?

- Where have I given up too soon when persistence was required?

- What would my life look like if I committed to disciplined, focused, persistent action for the next 30 days?

So build your discipline — even when it's hard.

Guard your focus — even when distractions come.

And persist — even when progress feels slow.

Because the promise belongs to those who refuse to quit.

You are closer than you think.

Keep going.

CHAPTER 11

The Terror Barrier — Breaking Through Your Internal Limits

Everything you've ever wanted is on the other side of fear.

— George Addair

You've built discipline. You've focused your attention. You've committed to persistence.

But now comes the real test — the one most people never talk about.

Let me give you a heads-up:

Right before a breakthrough, something strange almost always happens —
you hit a wall.

Not a physical wall — a mental and emotional one.

A wave of fear, anxiety, and resistance rises up out of nowhere. You question everything. You doubt yourself. It almost feels spiritual — because it is.

That's what's known as **the Terror Barrier** — a term coined by one of my mentors, the late Bob Proctor.

It's your mind's way of trying to protect you from the unknown. You're stepping out of your comfort zone — and your subconscious panics.

It floods you with thoughts like:

- "What if I fail?"
- "Who am I to do this?"
- "This is too risky."
- "What will people think?"

Sound familiar?

The Barrier Before Breakthrough

This is the moment that separates the committed from the curious.

Most people retreat.
They back off.
They shrink.

And often… they're just inches away from the very thing they've been praying for.

But hear this:

That fear? **It's not a red light.** It's confirmation.

It means you're doing something different.
It means you're stepping into the new — and your old programming doesn't like that.

Real Life: Mark Hits the Wall

Mark had always played it safe. Steady job. Reliable paycheck. Low risk, low stress.

But deep down, he had a dream — to start his own fitness brand and coach others toward the transformation he'd experienced.

He finally started moving on it. Registered the business. Posted content. Booked a few clients. He felt momentum building…

And then came the test.

He was offered a promotion at work:
More money. More security. Less time for his dream.

And suddenly, the thoughts came:

- "Maybe this is God telling me to stay put."

- "This coaching thing was probably just a phase."

He almost talked himself out of it.

But what Mark didn't realize was — he was bumping up against **the Terror Barrier.**

His old comfort zone was calling.

But he chose differently.

He pushed through the fear. He kept showing up. He kept building.

A year later, he was coaching full-time — and helping hundreds of people break through their own limits.

The fear wasn't a sign to quit. It was proof he was on the edge of breakthrough.

This Is Where Growth Happens

Every successful person you admire has faced this barrier.

This is where the masses turn around.

This is where the enemy whispers, "This is too much. You're not ready."

But it's not a sign to turn back.

It's a signal that you're on the right path.

Growth always comes with resistance.

The secret?

The only way past the Terror Barrier... is through it.

Feel the Fear — and Move Anyway

Courage isn't the absence of fear — it's choosing to act in spite of it.

You don't need to be fearless to move forward.
You just need to **trust what God put in you more than the fear that rises against you.**

2 Timothy 1:7 reminds us:

"For God has not given us a spirit of fear,
but of power, love, and a sound mind."

You are not your fear.
You are not your past.
You are not your limiting thoughts.

You are powerful. You are chosen. You are ready.

This isn't a step backward — it's a sign you're leveling up.

Take the Step

So what's your next move?

- Make the call.

- Launch the business.

- Write the book.

- Apply for the opportunity.

- Share the vision.

- Say yes to your next season.

You don't need permission — you need motion.

This is the turning point.

And the only way past the Terror Barrier... is through it.

So feel the fear — and move anyway.

Reflection & Journaling Prompt

- Where in your life have you hit a wall — and started to retreat?

- What dream or idea are you holding back on out of fear?

- What would it look like to move forward *anyway*?

- What's one bold step you can take this week — not because you feel ready, but because you're committed?

CHAPTER 12

Speaking Life — The Power of Affirmation and Daily Renewal

Words are free. It's how you use them that may cost you.

— KushandWizdom

Fear may be the barrier — but your **words** are the breakthrough.

Right after resistance shows up, the next battle often begins... internally.

And it starts with how you speak — especially to yourself.

The Bible doesn't downplay the power of words.

In fact, it elevates them:

"Death and life are in the power of the tongue, and those who love it will eat its fruit."

— **Proverbs 18:21**

Words create worlds.

And the words you speak — particularly the ones that never leave your own mind — shape the reality you live in.

That's where **affirmations** come in.

Affirmations Are Not Hype — They're Truth in Action

Affirmations are not hype.

They are **declarations** — **agreements with truth.**

They help rewire the subconscious by repeating what God says is true
until it becomes what **you** believe is true.

Affirmations remind you who you are — before the world tries to tell you otherwise.

Here are a few examples:

- I am created in God's image. I am not broken. I am whole.

- I am bold, focused, and consistent.

- I am a magnet for divine opportunities.

- God's favor surrounds me like a shield.

- I have the mind of Christ. I think clearly. I act courageously.

Repeat them daily — out loud. In the mirror. In prayer.
Write them on your bathroom mirror, your phone background, your journal.
Let them become the **soundtrack of your life.**

Want to take it further?

Write your own.

Base them on the very lies you've been believing — and speak the opposite.

If you've been thinking, *"I'm always behind"* — say:

"I am right on time. I am aligned with God's timing."

If you've been thinking, *"I'm not good enough"* — say:

"I am equipped, anointed, and chosen for this."

Your words are not decoration — they are design.

Renewing the Mind, Daily

Romans 12:2 puts it this way:

"Do not conform to the pattern of this world, but be transformed by the renewing of your mind."

That renewal?

It's not once. It's daily.

Every single day, you have the choice to agree with truth — or with fear.

To speak life — or to echo doubt.

Real Life: Jordan's Mirror

Jordan was going through a rough season.
A divorce, career changes, and an identity crisis all at once.

He felt lost — like the person he used to be was gone, and the one he was becoming didn't quite exist yet.

But something simple changed everything:
He started speaking life over himself.

At first, it felt ridiculous.
Standing in the mirror every morning, looking himself in the eyes, saying things like:

- "You're not done."

- "You're stronger than you feel."

- "God's not finished with you."

He didn't believe those words at first.
But he spoke them anyway.

Day by day, those words began to reframe his reality.
He stood taller. He thought clearer. He began to heal — and hope again.

Why?

Because he didn't just think about change. **He spoke it into being.**

Words have the power to create worlds.

And the words you speak — especially to yourself — shape the world you live in.

This is what this chapter is about:

Not just having faith — but **speaking like someone who does**.

Not just reading scripture — but **declaring it like a weapon**.

You were made in the image of a Creator who **spoke the world into existence**.

And His Word says **the kingdom of God is within you**.

So speak like it.

Reflection & Journaling Prompt

- What negative internal dialogue have I been repeating — and what truth do I need to speak instead?

- What are three affirmations I can start declaring daily?

- What scripture can I begin to speak over my life?

- How would my day feel different if I began it by speaking life over myself?

CHAPTER 13

True Success — God's Version vs The World's

Try not to become a person of success, but rather try to become a person of value.

— Albert Einstein

You've built a vision.

You've chosen faith.

You've taken action.

You've learned to show up with discipline, stay focused on what matters, and persist through resistance.

Now it's time to pause — and ask one of the most important questions on this journey:

What does success actually mean to you?

Because if *you* don't define it, the world will gladly do it for you.

And here's the warning:

"What good is it for someone to gain the whole world, yet forfeit their soul?" — **Mark 8:36**

If your version of success costs you your peace, your family, your identity, or your integrity…

is it really success?

You've got to be careful what you chase.
Because sometimes, in the pursuit of "more," we lose sight of what really matters.

That's why it's essential to **count the cost** — and build your life around the things that will still matter five, ten, even fifty years from now.

What the World Pushes — and Why It's Not Enough

From the time we're young, we're fed the same formula:

Hustle harder. Earn more. Look better. Climb higher.

Every commercial is selling that image.
Hollywood glamorizes it.
Social media magnifies it.
Marketing companies prey on it — convincing you that a better body, a faster car, or a bigger house equals a better life.

But here's the truth:

Success isn't just about what you achieve — it's about who you become in the process.

Real success is building a life that **feels good to live** — not just one that looks good on paper.

It's about setting meaningful goals that align with your values, your vision, and your Creator's wisdom.

This book isn't about playing small.
It's about helping you build something that *lasts* — and making sure it's *your* definition of success, not someone else's.

What the World Says vs. What Wisdom Teaches

The world says:

- Climb higher

- Be louder

- Chase status

- Accumulate more

But history — and wisdom — tells us something deeper.

The most impactful people in history weren't known for what they *owned*, but for **how they lived**.

They had clarity. Conviction. Depth. Integrity.

Jesus wasn't rich by worldly standards, yet He fulfilled His purpose perfectly.
Paul was imprisoned and persecuted, yet he called it joy.

That's because true success isn't about how high you climb
—

It's about how deeply you live in alignment with your calling.

You've probably felt this before:

You hit a milestone — a number, a raise, a big win — and instead of fulfillment, you feel... flat.
Empty. Unmoved.

That's because success isn't just about doing more — it's about doing **what matters most**.

"Seek first the kingdom of God and His righteousness, and all these things will be added to you." — **Matthew 6:33**

Whether or not you consider yourself deeply religious, this principle holds truth:

When your life is aligned with what matters eternally, the rest begins to fall into place.

That doesn't mean it will always be easy.
But it will be **real**. Sustainable. Fulfilling.

You can still build big.
You can still win.
But now it's from a place of **clarity** — not comparison.

Real Life: Alicia's Redefinition

Alicia built a business that checked all the boxes — multiple six figures, high-end clients, a beautifully curated social media presence.

But behind the scenes?

She was exhausted.
Her family life was strained.
Her mental health was slipping.

She had built a version of success that looked great to everyone else... except her.

So she stepped back.
She redefined what success meant to her:

- More time with her kids

- Space to think, pray, and be present

- Meaningful work that aligned with her values

She didn't give up on success — she just stopped chasing someone else's version of it.

And in the process, she finally felt the **peace and fulfillment** she'd been missing.

Ask Yourself:

- Are the goals I'm chasing actually mine — or just what I've been told to want?

- Am I measuring success by numbers… or by meaning?

- Am I living in alignment with who I say I want to be?

- What would it look like to succeed **without sacrificing** what matters most?

You can still go far.
You can still go fast.
But now, you'll go with clarity and peace — not pressure and pretense.

Reflection & Journaling Prompt

- Define success in your own words. What does it truly look like for you?

- Where in your life have you been chasing someone else's version of success?

- What would it look like to trade pressure for purpose?

- What's one area where you need to reset your definition of "winning"?

CHAPTER 14

Your Life, Your Design — The Final Word

Your life is your story. Write well. Edit often.

— Unknown

You've made it to the end of this book — but really, this is just the beginning.

If there's one truth I hope you carry forward, it's this:

Your life is what you make it. Nothing more... nothing less.

You are not here by accident.
You are not broken.
You are not too late.

Everything you've been through — the pain, the lessons, the false starts, and the growth — has been preparing you for this moment.
For this version of you.
The one who decides to believe again.
To stop settling and start building.
To live by design, not by default.

This book wasn't written to impress you.
It was written to **ignite** you.

I didn't grow up thinking I'd be an author.
I grew up just trying to survive.

But through faith, failure, persistence, and a whole lot of grace, I discovered something:

We were all created by a Creator.
And that means we were created to create.

My Intent in Writing This Book

I wrote this because I got tired of watching good people live small.
Tired of seeing potential go wasted because of fear, bad programming, or the belief that "this is just how life is."

I got tired of watching **faith be treated like a waiting room**, instead of the **launchpad** it was meant to be.

Faith moves.
It asks.
It seeks.
It knocks.
It builds.

And that's what I want for you.

This book is a **blueprint** — but you are the builder.

You've now seen the power of vision, the necessity of faith, and the irreplaceable force of action.
You've learned to ask boldly, seek intentionally, and knock relentlessly.

So what now?

Next Steps: How to Activate What You've Learned

Don't just read this and close the book.
Use it. Apply it. Let it transform the way you think, move, and live.

---

1. Reflect Weekly

Ask yourself:

- What did I believe this week?

- Where did I act in faith?

- Where did I hold back — and why?

---

2. Write Daily

Use these prompts to guide your thoughts and your day:

- What is my vision for today?

- What do I believe is possible?

- What am I asking, seeking, and knocking for?

---

3. Speak Life

Create affirmations rooted in scripture, identity, and truth.

Say them out loud — every single day.
Let them become your new internal language.

---

4. Revisit This Book Often

Don't treat this as a one-time read.

Come back to it.
Let it be your **playbook**, your **mirror**, your reminder of who you really are.

Final Word: You Were Made for More

If no one's told you lately — let me be the one:

I believe in you.
And more importantly, **God believes in you.**

The Creator placed greatness inside you — not to stay hidden, but to be brought forth.

So go build.

Go shine.

Go become who you were created to be.

And always remember:

Life is what you make it.

Nothing more… nothing less.

Reflection & Journaling Prompt: Make It Yours

This is your space.

Use it to process, dream, and hear from God.

Write your truth. Speak from the heart.

Let this be a sacred pause in the chaos of life.

◆ IDENTITY & BELIEF

- What beliefs have been holding me back?

- Who does God say I am?

- Where in my life have I been playing small?

◆ VISION & PURPOSE

- What future do I want to create?

- If I could design my life with no limitations, what would it look like?

- What has God placed on my heart that I haven't acted on yet?

◆ FAITH & ACTION

- What step of faith am I avoiding?
- What's one bold move I can take this week?
- What does "walking in faith" look like for me today?

◆ DISCIPLINE & MINDSET

- What daily habits will move me toward my vision?
- Where am I wasting focus or energy — and what needs to change?
- What does consistency look like in this season?

◆ SPIRITUAL ALIGNMENT

- What scripture speaks directly to where I am right now?
- What is God asking me to seek, ask, or knock on?
- What does success look like in the Creator's eyes — and how can I align with that?

Your Personal Declaration

Use this space to affirm who you are, what you believe, and what you're building.

Speak it. Write it. Live it.

I am

_____

I believe

_____

I will

_____

I am committed to

_____

Let's Stay Connected

If this book spoke to you, challenged you, or helped you reconnect with who you really are — I'd love to hear your story.

Whether it's your personal declaration, a breakthrough moment, or just a question that's stirring, feel free to reach out.

Email: contact@rayborell.com

Author Website: rayborell.com

Book Website: lifeiswhatyoumakeitbook.com

You were never meant to walk this journey alone.

Keep building. Keep believing. And keep becoming.

— Ray

www.ingramcontent.com/pod-product-compliance
Lightning Source LLC
LaVergne TN
LVHW051248080426
835513LV00016B/1806